little hands big sounds

exploring instruments

BY: MELISSA WHITTINGTON

THIS BOOK IS FOR ADDIE,
WHO WAS BORN TO MAKE
MUSIC.

Piano

Bing, bong black and White. Plays a happy tune just right!

Guitar

Strum it high or strum it low, Makes a catchy music flow!

Drum

Boom, boom boom it goes. Wiggle your happy toes and nose!

Violin

Squeak and sing, a funny sound, Makes happy music dance around!

Trumpet

Toot, toot, toot it goes. Makes a jazzy, brassy noise.

Flute

Hoo, hoo, hoo it blows, Soft and sweet the music goes!

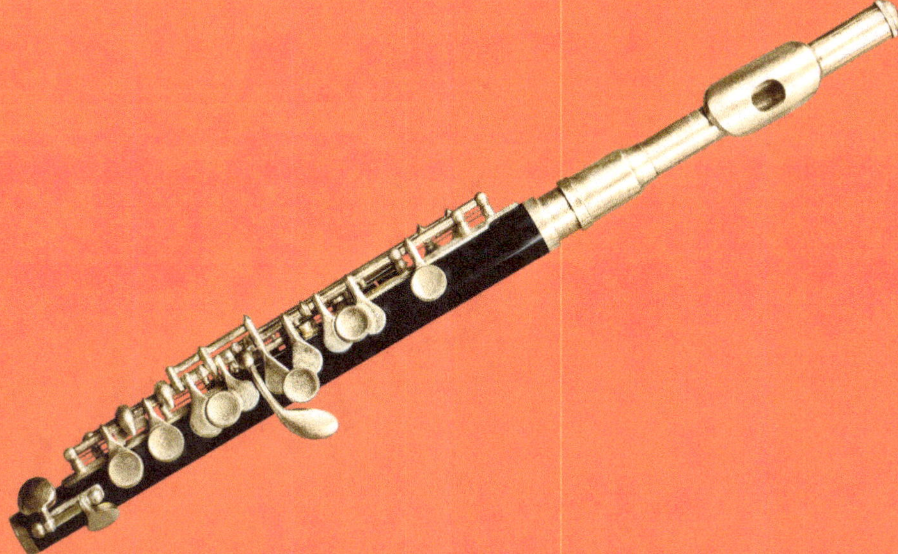

Saxophone

Saxy sounds so cool and bright, Makes you wanna wiggle left and right!

Ukulele

Hawaiian tunes and happy strum, Makes a song that's lots of fun!

Maracas

Shake, shake, shake and sing, Hear the happy shaky thing!

Cymbals

Clang, clang, cymbals crash, Makes a loud and happy clash!

Harp

Twinkle,
twinkle,
golden
strings,
Magical music
when the
harp sings!

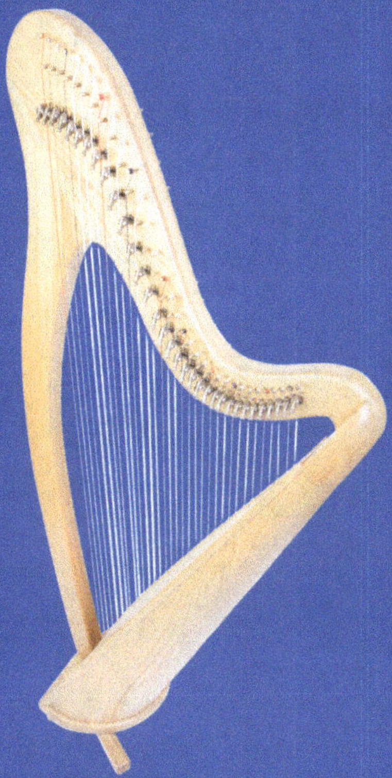

Cello

Big and tall
with a
rumbling
sound, makes
happy music
all around!

Clarinet

Tweet,
tweet, a
happy bird,
Plays a silly,
squeaky
word!

Triangle

Ting, ting, ting, the tiny thing. Watch me as I make it sing.

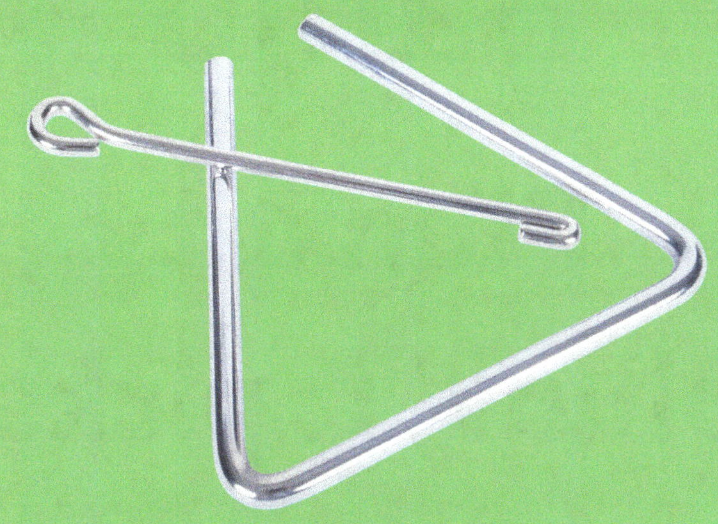

Banjo

Plunkety plunk, it picks and strums. Looks like a guitar mixed with a drum.

Tambourine

Jingle, jangle,
shake it high,
Makes a
party in the
sky!

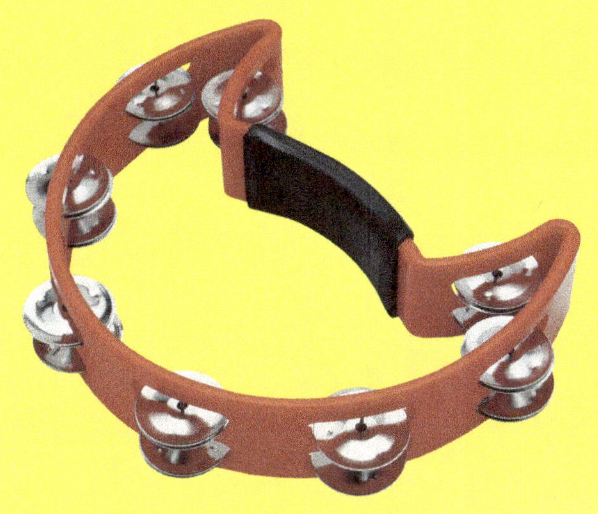

Accordion

Stretch and squeeze, it makes a whoosh, Polka Dancers feel the groove!

Congas

Bongo, bongo, here at last.

Use your hands and make it fast!

Good
Bye